D1390285

ROALD DAHL

# James and the Giant Peach: The Book and Movie Scrapbook

## *by* Lucy Dahl

DESIGN *by* Molly Leach  PHOTOGRAPHS *by* Lucy Dahl

PUFFIN BOOKS

PUFFIN BOOKS

Published by the Penguin Group
Penguin Books Ltd, 27 Wrights Lane, London W8 5TZ, England
Penguin Books USA Inc., 375 Hudson Street, New York, New York 10014, USA
Penguin Books Australia Ltd, Ringwood, Victoria, Australia
Penguin Books Canada Ltd, 10 Alcorn Avenue, Toronto, Ontario, Canada M4V 3B2
Penguin Books (NZ) Ltd, 182–190 Wairau Road, Auckland 10, New Zealand

Penguin Books Ltd, Registered Offices: Harmondsworth, Middlesex, England

First published in the USA by Disney Press, a division of The Walt Disney Company 1996
Published in Puffin Books 1996
3 5 7 9 10 8 6 4 2

Designed by Molly Leach

Made and printed in Great Britain by William Clowes Ltd, Beccles and London

*for* my father


— L. D.

# This
## is where it
## all began.

Every afternoon my father, Roald Dahl, strolled through our garden in England.

At the top of the garden, at the entrance to the apple orchard, stood this cherry tree. The blackbirds loved its fruit and gobbled it up before we ever saw a single cherry.

**This made my father hopping mad,** as he waved his walking stick in the air, furious with the pesky birds. As he searched within his mind for a solution to this problem, an idea began to form. As he said later in an interview, "It was a tiny seed of an idea. I walked around it, looked at it, and sniffed it for a long time. Why should the fruit stop growing at a certain size only to be eaten by greedy birds? What would happen if it didn't stop growing?"

And so the seed began to develop into a story.

His children loved his story, and so Roald Dahl began writing his first children's book, *James and the Giant Peach*. Why peach? What about the cherry? As my father said, "I thought, apple? Pear? Plum? . . . Peach is rather nice, a lovely fruit. It's pretty, it's big, and it's squishy. You can go into it and it's got a big seed in the middle which you can play with." That's simply the way it started.

**Not just the cherry changed form.**

> **But**
> Miss Spider was an ant,
> the Grasshopper was a froghopper,
> the Glowworm was a dragonfly,
> and the Ladybird was a beetle.

*Earwig* (

*Ant*

*Rose Chafer —*

*Assassin Bug — an efficient carnivore, hunts its living prey on trunks of trees.*

*Beetle — Ladybird Beetle. — All carnivorous, also vegetable matter. (Seven-spot ladybird)*

*The Devil's Coach-horse (Beetle) ... a threatening attitude and emits a smell.*

*The Rose Chafer (Beetle) one of the most beautiful.*

*Froghopper (Bug)*

**Dahl** was a thorough researcher. The insects that he eventually chose for the story are commonly found in and around the English countryside.

My father loved gardening, and with the help of an encyclopedia and the real-life insects, he was able to learn everything he needed to know, so that he could write with accurate detail of the creatures' habits. He studied them so thoroughly, he could create personalities that reflected their own insect lives.

**Every day** he walked from our house through the rose garden and up the fifty-yard path to his work hut. This peculiar little building was his office.

"My little nest," he called it.

# This is where he wrote all of his books . . .

as he sat in his mother's arm-chair, with a sleeping bag over his legs for warmth and his feet propped up on an old trunk filled with wood.

He always went to his hut from 10 A.M. to 12:30 P.M. and then again from 3 P.M. to 5:30 P.M. every day,

## including weekends.

# He kept his treasures on a table where he could see them:

A heavy **SILVER BALL** made from the inner wrappers of his weekly chocolate bar, from his school days. A **CEDAR CONE** and a carving of a **WHALE**, made from whale bone. A wooden carving of the **GRASSHOPPER**. A **ROCK** veined with opal, sent from a boy in Australia, after a school telephone/radio interview, where Dad asked the boy if he ever found any opals. "All the time," the boy replied. The head of a **FEMUR**, Dad's actual hip-bone, removed because of arthritis. A small model of a hurricane fighter **PLANE**. Little pieces of Dad's **BACKBONE**, restored in fluid, from a Laminectomy. **PETRIFIED ROCK** (1,000 years old)

# When I went away to

boarding school, he would write to me
twice a week. I loved his letters, and it
was comforting to imagine him in his
hut as he wrote funny poems to brighten
up the drudgery of my school days.

My father would often rewrite a single
page ten times, moulding and shaping
the story line and the characters

## until it was
## just right.

# JAMES AND THE GIANT PEACH

## 1

When James Henry Trotter was still only a tiny baby, his mother and father unfortunately got eaten up by an angry rhinoceros in the London Zoo. Ever since then, poor James had lived with his ▓▓▓▓▓▓ They were Aunt Sponge and ▓▓▓ker, and I ▓▓ say that they were both really horrible people. They were selfish and lazy and cruel, and they were continually beating poor James for practically no reason at all. They never called him by his real name, but always referred to him as "you horrid little beast," or "you filthy nuisance" or "you miserable creature", and they had never once given him a toy to play with, not even at Christmas. On his birthdays (if they happened to remember them) he would receive a pair of second-hand shoes that didn't fit, or an old raincoat far too big for him, or something equally sad.

They lived — Aunt Sponge and Aunt Spiker and James — in a queer ramshackle house on the top of a high hill in the south of The hill was so high that from almost anywhere in the garden James could look down and see for miles and miles across a marvellous

(no page)
The further in y safer you'll

have made — and a small boy to st he knelt down h head and shoulders
Now if only i make room for his
He crawled was rushing to stop Thought excitedly,
Behind sound of the old
hobbling up to the tunnel entrance "Ah, those pretty little c of the knife... just a come!... Where on earth
James damps and murky
The curious bitter-sweet smell of fresh under his knees, and peach juice James opened his on his tongue. It ta
He wa though the tunnel were the gigantic fruit

Told himself, The

(no para)

enough, perhaps, for
... and hide. Quickly
of it and poked his

in far enough to
body.
kept on crawling. There
... isn't a hole, he
tunnel!
... could hear the
footsteps as he came
went past it without seeing it
... shouting, "One slice
knees... and off they'll
boy got to?"
crawling. The tunnel was
around him there was
The floor was soggy
were wet and slicky,
... from the ceiling,
and could some of it
...

uphill one, as
it toward the very centre of
seconds, he paused and

out of

down
toward

---

...and ... waist.

poor long green shiny body tumbling over and
~~poor body Tumbling over and~~ over through space.
"Silkworm!" yelled James. "Quick! Start
spinning!"
The Silkworm sighed, for she was still very tired
but she did as she was told.
"I'm going down after him!" cried
James, grabbing the silk rope as it started coming
out of the Silkworm. "The rest of you hold onto Silkworm
so I don't pull her over with me, and later
on, when you feel three tugs on the rope, start
hauling me up again."
He jumped, and he went tumbling
down through the air after the Caterpillar, down, down, down
toward the sea below, and you can imagine how quickly the
Silkworm had to spin to keep up with the
speed of his fall.
"We'll never see either of them
again!" cried the Ladybird. "Oh, dear! Oh, dear!
just when we were all so happy, too!"
But half an hour later, there came
three tugs on the rope. "Pull!" shouted the
Earwig. "Everyone get behind me and pull!" There
was about a mile of rope to be hauled in,
but they all worked like mad, and in the end,
over the side of the peach, there appeared a
dripping wet James with a dripping wet Hang-

# Almost everything that he wrote about had influenced his life in some way.

Aunt Spiker and Aunt Sponge, for example, were a foul mixture of his cruellest teachers throughout his school days. The Cloud-Men were derived from a tree in blossom. "Close your eyes," Dad said, as we walked through the orchard in spring. Then he led me to the blooming tree. "Now open them," and all I could

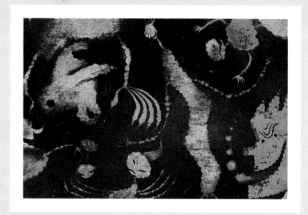

see were little faces in what appeared to be clouds in the sky.

The house where James lived with Aunt Spiker and Aunt Sponge, however, did not have any similarities to our family home.

We lived in a rambling Georgian farmhouse, nestled within the English countryside. Each room seemed to connect to another. It was the type of house in which friends who came to visit sometimes got lost.

More often than not, a quick trip to the bathroom became an unexpected adventure. Not only because the probability of finding your way back was low, but because you would find yourself surrounded and intrigued by little treasures.

# The house was filled

**with books,** rare paintings, photographs taken during World War II, baskets of golf balls, walking sticks, poems, literary awards, Wellington boots, drawings of peaches, grasshoppers and ladybirds, witches, twits, and chocolate.

Many of the paintings and sketches that were sent to my father from children through-out the world were stuck on the walls with strips of tape, in a kind of ever-changing gallery.

# Each letter or drawing that came to the house was acknowledged with a poem of thanks.

My teacher loved using the cane.
He would thrash me again and again.
I'd be raised in the air
By the roots of my hair
While he shouted, "It's good for the brain!"
--------------------
I used to wear pants extra thick
To lessen the sting from his stick,
When he saw what I had done
He yelled, "This is no fun!"
"Take them off altogether and quick!"
From your letters to me it would seem
That your teacher is clearly a dream.
There's no whacks on the bum
When you can't do a sum,
Instead you get strawberries and cream.

My teacher wasn't as nice as yours seems to be,
His name was Mr. Unswur and he taught us history,
And when you didn't know a date he'd get you by the ear
And start to twist while there you sat quite paralyzed with fear.
He'd twist and twist and twist and twist it more and more,
Until at last the ear came off and landed on the floor.
Our class was full of one-eared boys, I'm certain there were eight,
Who'd had them twisted off because they didn't know a date.
So let us now praise teachers who today are so fine.
And yours in particular is totally divine.

--------------------

As I grow old and just a trifle frayed,
It's nice to know that sometimes I have made
You children and occasionally the staff
Stop work and have instead a little laugh.

Every day, boxes of fan mail came to
our house, and one of the most
frequently asked questions was,

## "WILL JAMES AND THE GIANT PEACH ever be a movie?"

The reply was always the same,

## "How?"

How could this wonderful story,
vivid within the imagination of
millions of children, be constructed
into a visual reality?

# So it was

with a great deal of nervousness and curiosity that years after JAMES AND THE GIANT PEACH was written I visited Skellington Studios in San Francisco, California, to see its filming begin. As I climbed to the top of the stairs, I saw a massive pinboard filled with

sketches and paintings of peaches, seagulls, insects, and, of course, Aunt Spiker and Aunt Sponge. It looked uncannily similar to our walls at home in England. As I was led from room to room of what looked like a giant warehouse...

KELLY A. ASBURY -'95

…I watched with amazement as the artists took the characters, the landscapes, and the story line I knew so well from my childhood, and moulded them into visual movie form.

JAMES AND THE GIANT PEACH was being shot as a movie using stop-motion animation. Part of this process involves using puppets with metal skeletons (called armatures) that are skillfully manipulated by the animators from one movement and one movie frame at a time to create a performance.

James and his insect friends were as much a part of my family as our beloved dogs, and now I realized that the animation artists had grown up with JAMES, too, and many of them were the same children whose sketches and paintings filled our house when I was a child.

Spending time in Skellington Studios, watching JAMES AND THE GIANT PEACH become a movie, was like stepping right into a world my father had created in words—only now the words were people, puppets, drawings, and movie sets.

James and the Giant Peach

Screenplay
by
Jonathan Roberts, Karey Kirkpatrick, Steve Bloom,

based on the book
James and the Giant Peach
by
Roald Dahl

Every movie begins with a script...

Then, because this movie is part action as well as stop-motion animation, the roles of the characters had to be cast.

The director, Henry Selick, flew from California to England in search of the perfect James.

PAUL TERRY

He interviewed five hundred young boys between the ages of seven and twelve.

After weeks of auditioning, Paul Terry was chosen.

Paul had never been in a film before.
He had only acted in his school plays.
Now he had to miss two months of school.

He kept up with
his studies with
a private teacher.

The insects were cast
in a very different way.

The process started with Lane Smith's designs . . .

EARTHWORM

GLASSES CAN CHANGE WITH DIFFERENT EXPRESSIONS

PUT ON MONOCLE AND BLACK EYE INSTANTLY TURNS WHITE

L.S.

HENRY: DIXIE STRAW STYLE ? L.S.

SUNGLASSES

Pretzel

SNAIL-LIKE EYES EITHER BLACK LIKE THIS OR REVERSED

SHOULD TRAIGHT LIKE THIS TOO STYLIZED

THIN ANTENNAE WITH NO BALLS ON ENDS OR CURLIQUES TOO CUTE.

REAL THIN HAIR NOT SCULPTED

THIN WIRE ARMS WHICH MEET AT THE SHOULDER

PER HENRY

2 FINGERS 1 THUMB 1 SLEEVE

REAL BULB (PREFERABLY AN ANTIQUE THIN GLASS ONE)

SPIDER

SOS

BOOTS

LOTHES HOULD MULATE N SECT'S ODY EGMENTS

EARTHW

LITTLE TEETH

'ARROW' NOSE

HAMMERHEAD SHARK

CENTIPEDE HEADS

WITH NOSE (LIKE A 2-D-ARROW)  HAT

MINUS HAIRS  BALD

SHORT LEGS

BEST TOMATO

MATRONLY

SKELETONS  MEDALS

PARROT

PEG LEG

SHARK BITE

Lane Smith #3

LADY BUG  FRONT

BACK

JAMES

# The designs were then sculpted . . .

## the clothes and props were made . . .

and the filming was ready to begin.

# The live-action segments

of JAMES AND THE GIANT PEACH were filmed at two separate locations. All of the scenes set in England were filmed in an old, vacant warehouse. The others were filmed at two naval bases in San Francisco.

Inside the warehouse a heavy mist hung in the air. At the base of a man-made hill was a picket fence.

At the top of the hill there was half of a house. There were windows, a front door, and even a roof, but it looked as if someone had just chopped the back section off. Since only the front of the house would be filmed, that is all that was built.

# In another section

of the warehouse was JAMES'S attic bedroom.
It was built with only three walls, similar to a doll's house,
with the front panel removed so there could be additional
space for unobstructed filming.

The walls were grey brick, constructed from rough
cement, and the floor was splintery wood. Above the
wrought-iron bed were cobwebs hanging from beams.

High in the wall opposite the bed was a small window with torn lace curtains, and below that stood a rickety wooden chair.

James had always seemed very real to me, and now, as I looked into the bedroom, there he was—the saddest, loneliest, most unhappy boy in the world.

# In yet another

section of the warehouse a large hill was built, and halfway down was a small peach tree without any leaves or blossoms. The first time I visited the warehouse, there were Aunt Spiker and Aunt Sponge sitting under the tree, reciting my favourite childhood poems.

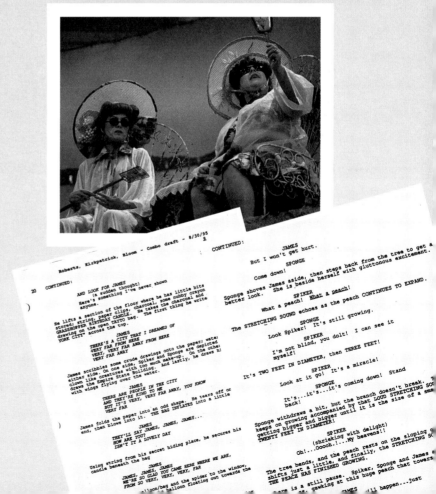

They looked
and sounded
exactly as I
had always
imagined
them.

Exactly as my
father described them.

4    CONTINUED:

Like a musical count-off, the fifth "WORK!" is the downbeat of...

THE WORK MONTAGE - **TITLE SEQUENCE**

5    CLOSE ON THE FRONT DOOR OF THE AUNTS RAMSHACKLE HOUSE.  The door
     flies open and A WOODEN CHEST ON WHEELS rolls out, the word
     "TOYS" emblazoned across it's front.  TILT UP to find James
     pushing the toy chest which is filled with rakes, hoes, shovels,
     etc.  He pushes it down the Barron, rocky hill to...

6    A SCRAGGLY PEACH TREE WITH NO FRUIT AND NO LEAVES.

James swings a pick axe at the dirt beneath the tree.  The film's
title appears beside this tableau:

                          **JAMES AND THE GIANT PEACH**

7    OMIT

8    OMIT

9    James polishes the grill of a 1936 Jaguar until it is shining
     like new.  PULL BACK to reveal the rest of the car is all rust.

10   OMIT

11   James pulls laundry from a basket and hangs it on a clothesline
     to dry.  First he pulls up Sponge's extra large girdle, then
     like scarves out of a magicians hat, he pulls out Spiker's long
     skinny gown -- which keeps coming, and coming, and coming...

12   James dusts a photo of Spiker and Sponge.  PULL BACK to find
     that the whole wall is covered with various photos of them.

13   EXT. AUNT'S HOUSE/BENEATH THE PEACH TREE - MORNING

A LARGE BUTTERFLY lands on a table beside a pitcher of lemonade.
SPLAT! - a hand-carved flyswatter squashes it into oblivion.
(O.S. - we hear the SOUND of an axe CHOPPING WOOD).

                         SPIKER
              Ew.   Wouldn't want one of those
              nesting in your knickers.

With a grimace, SPIKER flicks the flyswatter and the bug flies
off.  It soars past Sponge who's so absorbed with her reflection
in her long handled mirror, she doesn't notice.

                         SPONGE
              I LOOK AND SMELL, I DO DECLARE
                AS LOVELY AS A ROSE
              JUST FEAST YOUR EYES UPON MY FACE,
                OBSERVE MY SHAPELY NOSE!
              BEHOLD MY HEAVENLY SILKY LOCKS...
              ...AND IF I TAKE OFF BOTH MY SOCKS
              YOU'LL SEE MY DAINTY TOES!

Although Aunt Spiker and Aunt Sponge are fictional characters, they reminded me very much of all the bullies I encountered as a child.

🍎 33

# Every morning I rode on

the school bus from our village to school. It was a half-hour journey and usually quite fun, until Lizzy came to our school. Lizzy was older than all of us. She intimidated us by walking menacingly down the aisle of the bus as she chose her victim for the day. She would yank a chunk of your hair back so hard that you instantly gave in to her demands. If you dared to say "no," she spat big globs slowly onto your face. We quickly learned to give her anything she wanted.

One evening during supper, I asked my father what he would do about Lizzy. The following morning, he handed me a piece of paper and instructed me to secretly teach the verse written there to everyone on the bus— except, of course, Lizzy. After a few days, and a lot of whispering, we were ready.

It was a frosty winter morning, and as my father took me to the bus stop, he wished me luck and drove away. On the bus, as expected, Lizzy walked down the aisle. She chose a small girl to pick on, and as she grabbed her hair and pulled it backwards, we all burst into song.

Why is Lizzy in a tizzy
On the way to school?
She makes a fuss upon the bus,
And acts just like a fool!

We cheered, we chanted, we clapped our hands, stamped our feet, and sang it over and over again until Lizzy was defeated.

She slumped into her seat, burst into tears, and begged us all to stop. It was our turn, however, and we didn't stop until we arrived at school.

The following morning, Lizzy climbed on the bus, sat quietly in her seat, and never hurt or bullied anyone ever again.

# In all my father's stories,

there are unexpected moments. Just when you think everything is running smoothly, something happens. This was also true during the filming of JAMES. The spider used in live action parts of the film was actually a baby tarantula. Its body was covered with a painted eggshell so she would match the sculpted spider used during the stop-motion segments.

Paul Terry, who was playing James, had to take the live tarantula carefully off her web and carry her across the room while singing a song.  This was a very brave stunt for a young boy, and at the end of one take, she bit his finger, leaving two painful red marks from her fangs.

## Both Paul and Miss Tarantula went home early that day.

Another unexpected moment was when my two children were invited to be a part of their grandfather's story.

# My father taught us that magical surprises are everywhere.

If you just look and listen, "extraordinary things will happen." Sometimes you can feel it or touch it or smell it—even taste it. But best of all is when you actually *see* magic— which we did on the set the day the peach was to break free and roll down the hill.

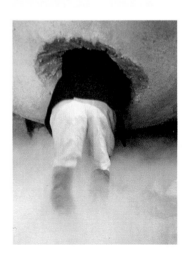

When all of the live filming involving the peach was complete, it was time for it to roll down the hill and squash the two aunts in their car. Most scenes can be reshot until they are perfect, but not this one. Since the peach would be destroyed during this scene, we all knew this was a one-chance, get-it-right, first-time-or-no-time shot.

A huge crane with a semicircle attachment was positioned at the bottom of the hill in order to catch the peach.

Six men were needed to push the peach free and set it off in the correct direction. After hours of careful planning, everything appeared to be ready.

I carefully chose my position to photograph the stunt. Aunt Spiker and Aunt Sponge were in the car, the cameras were rolling, the stunt coordinator had given us all a briefing on where to run if the peach went the wrong way.

# Suddenly, there was a loud SNAP!

And without any warning or pushing from the crew, the peach crashed through its fence and began rolling down the hill, heading directly for Aunt Spiker and Aunt Sponge's car.

It was out of control, but amazingly on course and inches before it hit the car, the peach came to a complete stop right in the arms of the crane.

We all looked at Henry, our director, for an explanation. He simply smiled, shrugged his shoulders and exclaimed,

# "That peach is ALIVE!"

# While the live-action sequences were being shot,

the artists at Skellington Studios in San Francisco were busy preparing for the stop-motion filming. This process involves puppets that are filmed while still. The puppet is positioned and filmed, then moved a fraction and filmed again. Eventually, when the frames are put together, the illusion of movement is created.

The stop-motion animator is responsible for creating the personality and movement of the puppets. For each puppet, a skeleton is built first. The arms, the legs, the ears, the smile, the nose, and the eyes all must move. Because so many emotions must be shown, different faces are made to create different expressions.

Each skeleton has an average of 150 pieces. The joints must fit together precisely, allowing the puppet the fullest possible range of motion when it is finished and dressed.

Pieces of wire connect all the movable parts. The skeleton (also called the armature) is then covered with rubber latex skin.

Then it is dressed. The costumes are made from hand-painted fabric and sewn together by hand.

Since continuous movement breaks down the rubber latex, each puppet has to be made about thirty-five times to have enough for an entire movie.

The biggest challenge in stop-motion animation is to make the characters look alive. Each scene is carefully planned and timed using a stopwatch. It takes about 400 frames or individual photographs to make a fifteen-second movie segment. Typically forty-five seconds of the movie are completed each week.

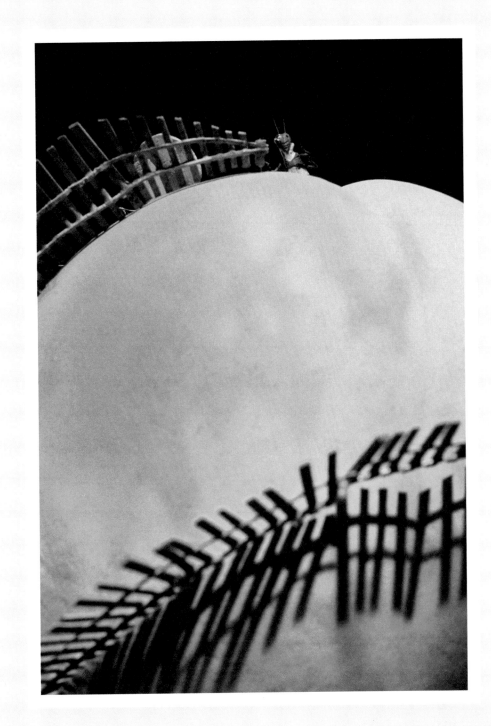

Although the screenplay of a movie based on a book is often very different from the original book, in the case of JAMES AND THE GIANT PEACH, Roald Dahl's writing was often used verbatim. We can follow a particular scene by

## looking at the manuscript, then the song, then the storyboard, and finally looking at Mr. Centipede himself!

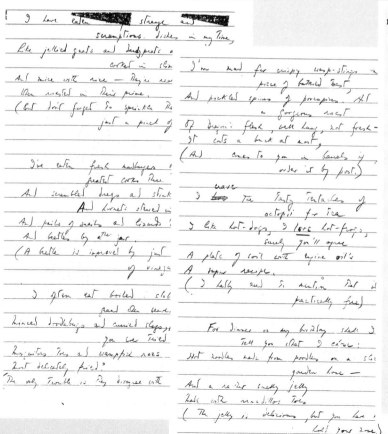

1800  SONG  "EATING THE PEACH"

CENTIPEDE
I'VE EATEN MANY STRANGE AND SCRUMPTIOUS
DISHES IN MY TIME,
LIKE JELLIED BUGS AND CURRIED SLUGS
AND EARWIGS COOKED IN SLIME,
AND MICE WITH RICE IS VERY NICE
WHEN THEY'RE ROASTED IN THEIR PRIME.
BUT DON'T FORGET TO SPRINKLE THEM
WITH JUST A PINCH OF GRIME.

Centipede prepares peach for the others during the instrumental segment. --

CENTIPEDE
I'M CRAZY 'BOUT MOSQUITOS
ON A PIECE OF BUTTERED TOAST
AND PICKLED SPINES OF PORCUPINES.
AND THEN A GREAT BIG ROAST
AND DRAGON'S FLESH, QUITE OLD, NOT FRESH--
IT COSTS A BUCK AT MOST...

GLOW-WORM
...A CUP OF TOAST.

JAMES GRASSHOPPER
EARTHWORM AND LADYBUG
IT COMES TO YOU IN BARRELS
IF YOU ORDER IT BY POST.

GRASSHOPPER
FOR DINNER ON MY BIRTHDAY
SHALL I TELL YOU WHAT I CHOSE?
HOT NOODLES MADE OF POODLES
ON A SLICE OF GARDEN HOSE-
AND A RATHER SMELLY JELLY
MADE OF ARMADILLO'S TOES.

Grasshopper holds his nose.

GRASSHOPPER
THE JELLY IS DELICIOUS,
BUT YOU HAVE TO HOLD YOUR NOSE.

Grasshopper lets go on "NOSE.". Background "Peach, peach"

Instrumental segment.

LADYBUG
I CRAVE THE TASTY TENTACLES
OF OCTOPI FOR TEA.
I LIKE HOT-DOGS, BUT I LOVE HOT-FROGS,
AND SURELY YOU'LL AGREE
A PLATE OF SOIL WITH ENGINE OIL'S
(MORE)

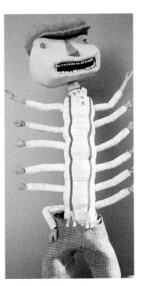

The question of how JAMES could ever be a movie was gradually being answered before my eyes. Stop-motion animation was part of the answer. Using Dahl's own words was another part and never forgetting the importance of imagination was the key.

In the book James's dream is to go to the Empire State Building in New York City.

The movie set was a towering illusion of the city.

At one end of a street stood a bright green 1930s truck, and on its wooden flatbed rested the giant peach.

The peach was almost as high as the buildings. A long wooden ladder leaned against it.

My favourite prop, the five-gallon buckets full of peach goop, contained a revolting mixture of peach pie filling, molasses, and water, mixed to perfect dumping consistency.

The movie took a different twist from the book when Aunt Spiker and Aunt Sponge followed James to New York.

Spiker and Sponge were cruel, selfish, and greedy adults who hated children and had no compassion for their difficulties in a world of grown-ups, bullies, teachers, rules, homework, punishments, and school.

## My father taught us that grown-ups don't always have the answers.

### I hated homework

and one Saturday morning I asked my father to help me with an idea for my English essay.

He leaned back in his big arm-chair and told me that he needed to think about it. I was a little surprised, as he usually had a number of funny ideas on the tip of his tongue. That afternoon he went to his work hut as usual.

As always, he emerged from his hut at 5:30 P.M., and found me in my room. He dropped two pieces of paper on my bed and as he left the room he said, "There's your story."

I was thrilled—all I had to do was rewrite it in my handwriting. It was brilliant. He was brilliant and I was sure to get an A+!

A few days later our essay books were returned to us. With complete confidence I opened mine, fully expecting top marks. To my horror, my teacher had given me a big red C- with a comment that read,

"You can do better."

When I complained to my father, he handed me another piece of paper; his school report card from when he was thirteen years old. Under English Composition it said he was thirteenth out of sixteen boys and although he didn't

"express himself badly," he was "apt to get muddled in his facts."

# ST. PETER'S, WESTON-SUPER-MARE.

Easter Term, 1928.

Name .....Dahl..... Form V. Number of Boys 16. Average Age 13.¼ Place in Form 12.

| SUBJECT | Order. | REMARKS. | Master. |
|---|---|---|---|
| SCRIPTURE - - | 11 | Fair. | F.J.A.D. |
| HISTORY - - | 10 | Appears interested and keen. | F.J.A.D. |
| ENGLISH GRAMMAR - | | Seems anxious to do well. | C.L.R. |
| ENGLISH COMPOSITION ENGLISH LITERATURE - | 13. | Does not express himself badly, but in reproducing a story is apt to get muddled with his facts. Very good | S.L. |
| GENERAL KNOWLEDGE | | | |
| GEOGRAPHY - - | 2 | Very good. | J.H.C |
| LATIN - - - | 13. | Has worked hard, & considering the fact that he is new to much of the V form work has done very creditably. | S.L. |
| GREEK or GERMAN - | | | |
| ARITHMETIC - - | 8 | Very satisfactory | J.H.C |
| ALGEBRA - - | 13 | ) | J.H.C |
| GEOMETRY - - | 13 | } very promising. | |
| FRENCH - - | 9 | Has done better this term. | J.H. |
| MUSIC | | His work has considerably this term | G.C.D |
| BOXING | | | |
| GAMES | | | |
| SECTION | | A very useful member indeed. | V.E.C. |
| HOUSE | | Conduct very good. | |
| GENERAL | | His work is good. | |
| | | Considerably above the standard of his age. | |

Boys return on .....Tues. May 1ˢᵗ..... 1928.

H. J. H. Francis

Anyone who has ever read—or, now, seen—JAMES AND THE GIANT PEACH knows that Roald Dahl never got muddled in the facts that mattered. The magic that had always worked on me and the millions of children who read his books has continued in the movie. Perhaps the best answer to the question of how could JAMES AND THE GIANT PEACH be a movie is the simplest: To Believe.

My father once wrote,

"Above all, watch with
glittering eyes the whole
world around you,
because the greatest
secrets are always hidden
in the most unlikely
places. Those who don't
believe in magic will
never find it."

Lucy Dahl remembers her father getting countless letters from children who all loved *James and the Giant Peach*. When meeting the people who worked on the film, she was touched and amazed to discover that they, as children, had been among those who had written to Roald Dahl. Ms. Dahl grew up in Buckinghamshire, England, and now lives in Martha's Vineyard, Massachusetts, with her two daughters, Phoebe and Chloe.

ROALD DAHL WITH DAUGHTER
LUCY IN 1973.

ROALD DAHL (RIGHT) WITH
WALT DISNEY DISCUSSING A
POSSIBLE MOVIE IN 1942.